EXCELLENCE IN POLICING

Simple Ways to Exceed Citizen Expectations in Every Encounter

ANDY HARVEY

Sarah —

When we look up Excellence there's a picture of you!

in the dictionary!!

Enjoy the book!

AHarvey

ISBN: 0692844724
ISBN-13: 978-0692844724

DEDICATION

I dedicate this book to my beautiful family, my wife Leticia, daughter Samantha, and son Jacob. Thank you for allowing me to chase my dreams. This is for my mother, Amelia, who was my greatest influence and passed away more than 20 years ago. I wrote a book, Mom! Te extraño mucho. My dad, Andy Sr., the toughest man I know and gave everything to make our lives better. Thank you, Dad. I wrote a book! My brother Jesse and sisters Carol and Liz, who still encourage me today- I love you dearly. To my Circle of Trust, you know who you are- abrazos. And always, to Father God for His favor, grace, and mercy.

ANDY HARVEY

CONTENTS

"MY SMALL CONTRIBUTION TO THE MOST NOBLE PROFESSION IN THE WORLD"

Policing in today's society is more complex and the demands placed on both officers and administrations require us to redefine what it means to be a professional. Excellence in Policing outlines how to add value to each police-citizen encounter. Our officers have used these lessons to increase the standing and legitimacy of our agency in our community. I strongly encourage every department leader to make EIP a must read!

Chief Dan Carolla,
Lake Dallas Police Department,
Lake Dallas, Texas

Today, perhaps more than ever before, each interaction between officers and the citizens they serve has the ability to set the trajectory of an entire profession. It is imperative that every man and woman who wears a badge understands this, and Chief Harvey's message will help to ensure that they do. Though the principles put forth in Excellence in Policing are timeless, this book will expose police executives and line officers alike to them in a fresh and easily digested manner.

Chief Emmitt Jackson
Keene Police Department
Keene, Texas

Sir Robert Peel's

Principle 1 "The basic mission for which the police exist is to prevent crime and disorder."

Principle 2 "The ability of the police to perform their duties is dependent upon public approval of police actions."

Principle 3 "Police must secure the willing cooperation of the public in voluntary observance of the law to be able to secure and maintain the respect of the public."

Principle 4 "The degree of cooperation of the public that can be secured diminishes proportionately to the necessity of the use of physical force."

Principle 5 "Police seek and preserve public favor not by catering to the public opinion but by constantly demonstrating absolute impartial service to the law."

Principle 6 "Police use physical force to the extent necessary to secure observance of the law or to restore order only when the exercise of persuasion, advice and warning is found to be insufficient."

Principle 7 "Police, at all times, should maintain a relationship with the public that gives reality to the historic tradition that the police are the public and the public are the police; the police being only members of the public who are paid to give full-time attention to duties which are incumbent on every citizen in the interests of community welfare and existence."

Principle 8 "Police should always direct their action strictly towards their functions and never appear to usurp the powers of the judiciary."

Principle 9 "The test of police efficiency is the absence of crime and disorder, not the visible evidence of police action in dealing with it."

INTRODUCTION

Every police-citizen encounter is a commercial that represents you, your agency, and police officers across this great nation. Just turn on your television or your phone and you will probably see an encounter that, from a citizen's viewpoint, didn't go very well. You probably do not like the thought of appearing in any commercial, but today's police officers don't have a choice. The good news is that you get to be the director of every one of your commercials. And just like directors who guide their cast members towards a well thought out vision, police officers should 'direct' (guide) those they encounter towards a safer and a fairer outcome. You will probably never receive an award for Best Director, but you didn't sign up for the recognition. This is because you're a servant at heart which drives you to be your very best to positively impact others.

Even though your intentions are good, there may be times when your 'commercial' doesn't come across well to your audience. The focus of this book is to help you gain a healthier understanding of how citizens may perceive the police. You will learn what is most important to citizens when dealing with the police and what they expect from you (the police). Just a note, the words you, us, we, and police are interchangeable throughout the book. These simple concepts presented here will help you more effectively manage perception during your citizen encounters that will increase citizen satisfaction and, more importantly, keep you and your fellow officers safer.

In this fast paced and technologically advanced world, the police need to keep up and find ways to not only remain relevant, but to stay ahead of society's demands and expectations. In other words, it's time to swap the checker board for the chess board. Consider this, chess forces you to be objective. [i] To be objective is to not be influenced by personal feelings, interpretations, or prejudiced, rather based on facts. [ii] Secondly, chess challenges players to think strategically. To be successful, you must be able to see at least 2 or 3 moves in advance to make the best decision NOW. These principles can and should be applied to policing. Although what the police do every day is certainly not a game, we can learn some lessons from chess that can be practical to every police-citizen encounter.

I have no doubt that you are proud to be a police officer and want the very best for you and your fellow officers, your families, and our country. You wouldn't have chosen this profession if you didn't hold these values in high regard. Many of you have also served our country in the military and have experienced war first hand. Whether you served directly in battle or served in a support role, you are a patriot and a servant. The sacrifices you and your family endured should never be forgotten.

But now you're serving our country here at home on the front lines protecting our democracy. Whether you're a veteran or not, we are all part of something bigger in our homeland. I believe the police are the fabric that holds our country together and helps make the United States the greatest nation in the world. Our nation is certainly not perfect. But I am proud to say that it's pretty damn good. Our country has gone through some challenging times recently. It's not the first time and it definitely won't be the last. Fortunately, our country is resilient and will rise in midst of this or any other crisis.

I am a firm believer that a crisis brings opportunity; these are times the police should not allow to pass by without affecting positive change in our nation. Yes, it's not just the police that must change, it's everyone. But let's focus on what we (the police) can control by using our influence and lead the way. Let's continue showing the world why police officers represent the very best in people.

Excellence in Policing is divided into several different concepts that include excellence, community expectations, legitimacy, procedural justice, authority, and more. These ideas will be discussed individually first and then collectively in order to illustrate their importance and relevance to policing today. At the end of each chapter, you will find Excellence Keys that serve as a quick review of the main points for that chapter.

Thanks for choosing to take this journey with me and countless fellow officers around the country who have heard this message and applied these principles immediately. If you can improve in just one area, then the journey is worth it. You, our communities, policing, and our country will be better for it.

LET'S GO.

CHAPTER 1

WHY EXCELLENCE IN POLICING?

I value excellence. I love what it stands for- extraordinary, class, fineness, brilliance, distinction, greatness, high worth, and quality, to name a few. I also value policing. I love what it represents- service, duty, authority, strength, honor, commitment, and justice. So, it makes sense to connect two things I hold in high regard to try and make a difference in your life and the lives of those we serve.

Excellence is a mindset, a lifestyle, a decision. It demands relentless effort, a laser focus, and strong attention to detail. A commitment to excellence is what separates goodness from greatness. The opposite of excellence is mediocrity, average, and doing the bare minimum because it's good enough. Today's policing requires us to be better than that, and rightfully so, if we are going to move forward with greater success.

> "A commitment to excellence is what separates goodness from greatness."

I am confident you value excellence, or you wouldn't be reading this book. Our profession is way too meaningful to the success of our great nation for the police to be anything but excellent. Mediocrity has no place in policing. The police simply cannot afford to be average. People depend on you to be excellent.

Notice I didn't say people expect you to be perfect; that's impossible. The great Vince Lombardi said, "Perfection is not attainable, but if we chase perfection we can catch excellence."[iii] Just as sharpshooters aim for the bullseye, we can zero in, align our sight, and achieve excellence. Policing is not a perfect science; dealing with human beings never will be. Errors will be made, but excellence requires zealous learning to overcome and minimize mistakes to progress as individuals and as a profession.

"Policing is not a perfect science, dealing with human beings never will be."

One of the United States Air Force Core Values is 'EXCELLENCE IN ALL WE DO.' I love that (you guessed it, I have Air Force blood). Excellence is part of the Air Force culture. It's no coincidence that #1: The United States Air Force is the best in the world and #2: the USAF strives for Excellence- not only in some things, but in ALL things. Ask any airman, from top to bottom, and he/she will be able to recite the USAF core values. For our Air Force, and in every branch of our awesome military, excellence is the only way to conduct business. Imagine what our world would look like if our military was mediocre. Don't you expect our military to be the very best? The same can be applied to law enforcement. The impact and influence we have on our nation should never be discounted. Citizens expect you to be the very best; they expect you to be excellent.

I am not suggesting that the police haven't been successful. We absolutely have on many levels. What got us to this level of success, however, will not take us to the next one. Policing should have a culture of excellence. Every officer in your department, from the recruit to the Chief, should be striving for 'Excellence in All They Do.' This excellence mindset is the catalyst that will push us to remain not only relevant in our nation but continue to be the very best in the world.

"What got us to this level of success will not take us to the next one. Policing should have a culture of excellence."

If we get too comfortable celebrating the perceived successes we've had and don't build on that momentum, then policing will suffer. This is what happens to both people and organizations that do not sustain an elevated level of success. Once they've reached a level of accomplishment, complacency sets in. Everything seems to be working just fine, so employees continue doing business as usual. And there's the trap! Without even realizing it, the decline begins. It's subtle at first, but by the time anyone realizes it, the downward spiral is in full swing and the inevitable becomes reality. We must not allow that to happen to our profession!

Policing has experienced a period of success since the mid 1990's. Record crime decreases in our country has helped us achieve perceived successes. It's been referred to as The Great American Crime Decline in a book by Frank Zimring.[iv] By the way, I encourage you to read his book; it will challenge you to think differently about possible crime causations and crime fighting strategies that have been deemed successful. There's been much written about it and frankly, the crime declines have been good for political business. But if we are not careful, policing can also begin that downward spiral if we get too comfortable in the perceived successes we've been fortunate to have experienced. The time to move is NOW, *before* complacency sets in. It's time to play chess and think strategically about how we will move forward.

Excellence is continuously striving for improvement. It means constantly moving forward, refusing to stay stagnant. Remaining stagnant and still expecting different results is not insanity, it's flat out dumb. Yes, I said it, DUMB! And we are better than that, way better! Settling is not an option if you want to take our profession to the next level.

> "Staying stagnant and still expecting different results is not insanity, it's flat out dumb."

Excellence involves change, and you know how much police officers hate change. Maybe hate is too strong, but it's safe to say we certainly don't embrace change in our profession. Striving for excellence in policing, however, includes being open to change. As you well know, society is changing fast, and if we don't change with it, then we will become irrelevant and a hindrance to the success of our nation. Our nation deserves better. Our nation demands excellence.

Excellence is learned, much like leadership. You were not born excellent; you must become excellent (even though your mother thought you were perfect). Aristotle said, "Excellence is an art done by training and habituation. We do not act rightly because we have virtue or excellence, but rather have those because we had acted rightly. We are what we repeatedly do. Excellence, then, is not an act but a habit."[v] Building a habit is simply doing things repeatedly. If you're not careful, you can develop unhealthy habits in policing. And, breaking bad habits is much more difficult than building good ones.

"Excellence, then, is not an act but a habit." Aristotle

When striving for excellence in policing, we should begin by looking at the brutal facts of our current reality. This includes acknowledging that we may have learned some false belief systems along the way that have been accepted as truth, so it's quite possible you may be doing things that may, in fact, be hurting you and us. You must know where you are NOW to get to where you want to go.

Before moving on any further, I should warn you—being excellent will not be easy. It requires you to get out of your comfort zone. I appreciate what Jim Collins wrote in Good to Great when he referred to the Stockdale Paradox, "You must have the discipline to confront the most brutal facts of your current reality, whatever they might be."[vi] Even though Collins was writing about organizations, I believe these principles can be applied to both our lives and our profession. Again, begin by knowing your current reality. This self-awareness includes acknowledging the good, the bad, and yes, the ugly. If you are truly and brutally honest with yourself, and people of excellence are, then you will look at your current reality, as painful as it may be.

Later in Good to Great, Fred Perdue of Pitney Bowes described looking at the brutal facts this way, "When you turn over rocks and look down at the squiggly things underneath, you can either put the rock down, or you can say, my job is to turn over rocks and look at the squiggly things even if what you see can scare the hell out of you."[vii] Most people will look at the rock and put it right back, quickly. Why is that? Most people would rather not look at the ugliness that lies beneath. We, in policing, don't have that luxury of choosing to look or not, we absolutely must. Then we can either adjust or simply continue conducting business as usual and expecting different results. Now here's the famous Dr. Phil question, "How's that working out for you?"

Look, I understand that looking at the squiggly things can be disgusting and uncomfortable; but that's precisely the point. I want you to be uncomfortable enough to want to see the current climate to make the right adjustments to break through the challenges the police face today. Disgust is a powerful emotion, so use it as a catalyst to move towards changing both policing and our society for the better. See, if you're comfortable where you are, then you won't have a reason to change. Why would you? Getting out of your comfort zone requires that you first decide that you are uncomfortable. People of excellence will look closely, as agonizing as it may be, because they understand that it must be done to remove the 'squiggly things' from our lives and in our case, our valued profession.

Moving forward will not be easy, so be prepared. One biblical version describes progressing as *straining forward* in order to reach a goal.[viii] I thought about the word strain and had to look it up. Strain means pain, similar to what happens when a muscle is overused. The muscle becomes enlarged when it's used in an uncommon way, which results in pain. Striving for excellence will also cause pain because you will use 'muscles' that you may have never used or don't use often. But just as the athlete who wants to be the very best, you will have to endure some pain to achieve excellence in all you do. No pain, no gain! Although I've also heard this version, "no pain, no pain!" Funny, but the reality is that nothing without pain or sacrifice holds much value. And what you do as a police officer has extreme value and is worth the price.

Chapter One Excellence Keys

- ➢ Excellence is continuously striving for improvement and demands relentless effort, a laser focus, and strong attention to detail.

- ➢ Mediocrity has no place in policing.

- ➢ Policing is not a perfect science; dealing with human beings never will be.

- ➢ What got us to this level of success will not take us to the next one. Policing should have a culture of excellence.

- ➢ Society is changing and if the police doesn't change along with it, then the police will not only become irrelevant but also a hindrance to the success of our nation.

- ➢ Striving for excellence in policing includes being open to change.

- ➢ Excellence is learned, much like leadership.

- ➢ When we strive for improvement, we should begin by looking at the brutal facts of our current reality (remember the squiggly things).

- ➢ What you do as a police officer has extreme value and is worth the sacrifice.

CHAPTER 2

PEOPLE STILL BELIEVE IN YOU

When I meet officers around the country, they generally express a belief that Americans' respect for the police has all but vanished. While it's understandable to feel that way given today's climate, the fact is that right now officers are experiencing some of the highest marks as it relates to respect in several decades. Look at this Gallup Poll that was published October 2016.[ix]

AMERICANS WITH GREAT DEAL OF
RESPECT FOR POLICE

2015	2016
64%	76%

GALLUP

76% say they have "a great deal" of respect for the police in their area. This is up 12% (64%) from last year (2015) alone! To be fair, 2016 was an extraordinary violent year for officers, so Americans may be more sympathetic towards police right now. Either way, the fact remains that most people still respect and believe in the you!

Do you wonder how public perceptions of the police are formed? How much influence do you believe the media has on our profession? After all, the media seems to love covering police news stories and videos that portray the police in a negative light. Or, do you have enough faith that people will form their own opinions about the police based on their personal interactions and experiences with you?

When I ask officers what their main concerns are about today's policing environment, their mistrust of the media is always in their top two or three. Understandably so, since the media tends to focus on the negative stories a heck of a lot more than all the positive things occurring in policing every day. Since this is a major concern for many of you, I want to provide you with some facts to consider that may challenge your current perspective. I want you to be encouraged about the future of policing.

Year after year, polls show that the public still believes in and trusts the police way more than they believe the media. Look at this Gallup Poll and compare where police officers and journalists are listed regarding honesty and ethical standards.[x]

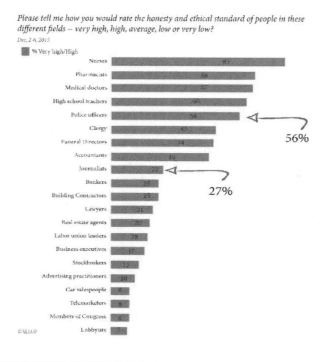

Please tell me how you would rate the honesty and ethical standard of people in these different fields — very high, high, average, low or very low?

"...the public still believe in and trusts the police way more than they believe the media."

Of those surveyed, 56% for the police compared to only 27% for the media is a stark difference and quite significant. This is important for you to know and always remember. When it comes to who the public trusts more, the police win every time! And honestly, it's not getting any better for the media.

"When it comes to who the public trusts more, the police win every time!"

Why do you think reporters always want to interview a uniformed police officer or want a departmental statement for their news stories? It brings credibility to their stories. Trust me; the media sees the same polls! Perhaps you (the police) give way too much credit to the media on how much they really impact public perception. Now, that's not to say the media doesn't have influence- it's just not as much as you may think. Stop worrying so much about the media and focus more on something you can control- YOU.

CHAPTER TWO EXCELLENCE KEYS

- ➤ Year after year, polls show that the public still believe in and trusts the police more than they believe in the media.

- ➤ When it comes to who the public trusts more, the police win every time!

- ➤ Stop worrying so much about the media and focus more on something you can control- YOU.

CHAPTER 3

DETAILS MATTER

"If you are going to achieve excellence in big things, you develop the habit in little matters. Excellence is not an exception, it is a prevailing attitude." Colin Powell

---

If excellence is found in the details, or as General Powell put it, in the "little matters," then how can we apply this concept to policing? I believe it's by focusing on the details of every police-citizen encounter. Recently, I decided to remodel my bathroom. When I say remodel, the entire bathroom was gutted, so I had to build it up from ground zero- floors, walls, everything. What the hell was I thinking? First problem, I've never done any of that type of work before. I've replaced a leaky faucet and done minor repairs but never anything to this extent. I had to learn how to do just about everything. Thank goodness for YouTube. I asked lots of questions, and I had to buy the right tools. Here's what I discovered through this long and tedious project.

Excellence is in the details. The important things like installing the vanity, sink, and general tile work weren't as difficult as I thought they would be. What did take lots of time and energy were those minute details. Features such as straight paint lines, matching knobs, caulking, and those small tile cuts are what gave me the most heartache. All of those trips between the bathroom and the wet saw to make just the right size cuts is more than I care to remember.

If I hadn't taken the time and dealt with the pains to make sure it was done properly; my project would've looked incomplete, maybe even sloppy. The bathroom would be functional, but that's about it.

That certainly wasn't my end goal. I wanted to build something I could be proud of, especially because only I knew how much work I had put into it.

Here is what I learned from this project and a few others since then:

1. Details Matter - Placing a heavy emphasis on the details helped me achieve excellence. These details added value to my home.

2. Functionality vs. Excellence - Functionality and excellence are two entirely different standards, and so are the results. Functionality is just good enough. Excellence is going above and beyond.

3. Right tools - Having the right tools was necessary to achieve my goal. I had to expand my toolbox with precise tools specifically designed for those excellent details that my hammer, screwdriver, or vice grips combo couldn't handle.

My lessons learned can also be applied to policing:

1. Details Matter - In policing, focusing on the details of every police-citizen encounter will help us achieve excellence. Excellence adds value to your community.

2. Functionality vs. Excellence - It's very possible for the police to provide basic services to the community while failing to add value and increasing public trust. Which one reflects your department?

3. Right tools - Adding tools to your police belt such as using more legitimate authority (also referred to as earned authority, covered in Chapter 6) and practicing procedural justice (Chapter 8), will help the police achieve a higher level of citizen satisfaction. The police can no longer use a hammer for everything.

In Chapter 4, we will dive into the details of every police-citizen encounter.

CHAPTER THREE EXCELLENCE KEYS

➢ Lessons about excellence can be applied to policing:.

✓ **Details Matter** - In policing, focusing on the details of every police-citizen encounter will help us achieve excellence and add value to your community.

✓ **Functionality vs. Excellence** - It's very possible for the police to provide basic services (functional) to the community while failing to add value and increasing public trust.

✓ **Right tools** - Adding tools to your police belt such as using more legitimate authority and practicing procedural justice will help the police achieve a higher level of citizen satisfaction.

CHAPTER 4

3 PHASE POLICE-CITIZEN ENCOUNTER MODEL

Citizens form their perceptions mostly based from their own individual experiences. In this chapter, let's get into the micro level (or the details) of policing by dividing police-citizen encounters into three phases- the Initial Contact, the Process, and the Outcome. My hope is that dissecting these encounters will give you an unfamiliar perspective and will make it easier to understand and apply the concepts in this book. *Excellence in Policing* focuses on what every police-citizen encounter may look like from a citizen's perspective. The main goal of this book is for you to gain a healthier understanding of how citizens *may* perceive you and what you can do to more effectively manage your encounters with the public. Thus, increasing the level of their satisfaction and forming positive public opinion as it relates to their experience(s) with you.

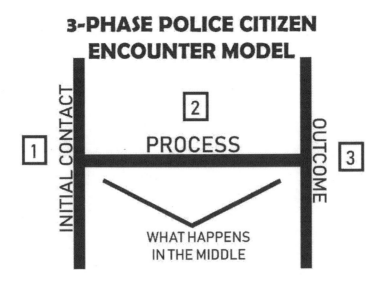

When I present my Excellence in Policing seminar to police officers and police leaders, I begin by asking them this question before delving into the phases, "Of these 3 phases, which one do you think is *MOST* important to citizens when it comes to their level of satisfaction of police service - the Initial Contact, the Process, or the Outcome?" Which one would you choose? I know- nobody likes these types of test questions. Keep in mind that they're *ALL* important to citizens, so you will be right whichever phase you choose. However, some of you will be a little more correct. ☺ Hold on to that thought for now.

The first phase is the *Initial Contact*. This stage can include a variety of things such as traffic stops, responding to a 911 call, or getting flagged down while you're walking into a Starbuck's *(my favorite place by the way)*. It also includes the reason for contact and whether the citizen initially believes it's legal or not. Remember, we are viewing this from a citizen's perspective. More importantly, it's where first impressions are formed by both parties. Citizens are sizing you up just the same way you do to them when you first meet. Both of you are probably asking the same questions such as, *"Who am I dealing with? Is he going to be cool or another asshole?"* First impressions are a fact of life; we all do it and that's okay. Remember that most citizens have a preconceived notion about you (police officers) already, and you've never even met! It may not be fair, but it's the truth.

If we are honest with ourselves (remember the squiggly things), the police can easily start off a citizen encounter on the wrong foot. The police may say the wrong thing, say something sarcastic (sarcasm will be covered later in Chapter 11) or maybe say nothing at all. Silence gives way too much room for a possible misunderstanding. A police officer's tone, body language, or mere presence can rub people the wrong way. Do you know any officers like this? I think we all do. Either way, there is some good news! If you start off on the wrong foot, YOU can make up ground during the next phase-the Process.

> "Sometimes, the police start a citizen encounter on the wrong foot.
> The good news is that YOU can make up for it during the Process."

The second phase is called the *Process,* or what I refer to as 'what happens in the middle.' It's what occurs between the Initial Contact and the Outcome of an encounter. This is when the officer's decision-making process begins to take shape and citizens' opinions are becoming solidified. Officers should pay close attention to this phase for several reasons. Again, if an officer begins the encounter (Initial Contact) negatively, the officer still can change the trajectory of the citizen's assessment of you. That is, if the officer redirects his actions intentionally and appropriately.

Later in the book, the concepts of managing perception and procedural justice will be discussed that will pertain mostly to this phase. For now, however, know that procedural justice means that citizens care more about how they are treated by authority figures than anything else. People want to be treated with a sense of fundamental fairness and with a level of dignity and respect. Furthermore, citizens' assessments about whether they were treated with fairness will predominantly depend on an officer's actions during the Process.

The final phase is the *Outcome.* This is the result of the police-citizen encounter or what you probably referred to as the disposition of the call. The Outcome can be anything from issuing a citation, making an arrest, or giving someone a warning, among other things. The Outcome will be viewed by the citizen as either favorable or unfavorable. This will depend on whether the citizen feels the violation (law) is legitimate (Chapter 7) *and* if the citizen perceives the officer's decision-making process was fundamentally fair. These concepts of legitimacy and procedural justice are the result of Tom

Tyler and Tracy Meares' research in these areas and will be expanded later in the book.

So back to the question I asked you about which phase is most important to citizens. Most participants choose either the Initial Contact or the Outcome as the most important phase. In actuality, the part that's most important to citizens is the Process, or what happens in the middle of the encounter. Admittedly, I was a bit surprised when I read the research. My belief system was flawed. By the way, I assumed the Outcome edged out the other phases.

Tom Tyler is a well-known researcher who wrote, *"...people will be concerned with whether they receive fair outcomes, arrived at through a fair procedure, rather than with the favorability of the outcomes.* [xi] In other words, *fairness* trumps even perceived favorable outcomes for citizens.

> "...fairness trumps even perceived favorable outcomes for citizens."

When I first discovered that a fair process was most important to people, I had an A-HA moment. Since I assumed that a favorable outcome would be most important to people, I wondered if other police officers thought the same way. And, if so, was there an opportunity for improvement in our profession? Consider this, if there is a substantial portion of police officers who aren't aware that how people feel they are treated by you is most important, then perhaps understanding the police-citizen encounter is an ideal area to focus on for both professional development and impacting our profession. I'm not referring to monumental changes in policing. I believe that merely moving policing one 'click to the right' has the potential to positively impact our profession and those we serve. Now that we are playing chess, then having an increased understanding of the human dynamic during every encounter is a must.

What if police officers treated the public believing that the Outcome was most important to citizens? With this approach, officers may not be too concerned with how they treat citizens throughout an encounter if the citizens receive a perceived favorable outcome. Have you ever heard an officer say, "I can't believe that lady complained on me, I gave her a warning! I knew I should have written her up!" These officers may be outcome minded. It doesn't take a rocket scientist to see how this can hurt efforts by the police to increase public community trust and confidence. This outcome mindset will hinder the ability for the police to exceed citizens' expectations during these encounters. Again, people care more about a fair process than even the outcome. I should emphasize that nothing is absolute when dealing with human beings, so please keep that in mind as we move forward.

In addition to fairness, people want to be treated with dignity and respect.[xii] Have you ever been thanked by an individual you arrested? I'm sure most of you have. If you haven't, do not put this book down! Why do you think that happened? Didn't you find it remarkable that someone would thank you after taking them to jail? More than likely, you treated this individual with a level of dignity and respect. You treated this person like a human being. Amid a very low time for that individual, you allowed that individual to keep their dignity. Chances are that person who thanked you may have dealt with the police before and his experience was much different with the previous officer(s). Perhaps that same officer was a business as usual type, robotic, or so cynical (Chapter 11) that he has become blind to the concept of respect, goodness, or fundamental fairness. Nevertheless, you did something different. I would say you performed your job with excellence. I realize it's difficult at times to treat some people with respect based on their behavior towards you. I get it, I've been there. Still, Excellence demands more from us; it demands we be the adult in the room, regardless of the situation.

"Excellence demands more from us; it demands we be
the adult in the room, regardless of the situation."

Being excellent in all you do can be a challenge at times. Remember what Aristotle said, *"Excellence is a habit."* It may not come easy, but the only way to develop a habit is by doing it repeatedly until it becomes *your* normal. Excellence in all you do is a habit. It becomes easier. You'll have some setbacks; you'll have some days when you will be less than excellent. That just means you're human! Again, excellence is not about perfection but about continuously striving for improvement. This means when we fail, and we will, we acknowledge it, learn from it, and drive on. You'll have an opportunity to be excellent the next encounter.

"The only way to develop a habit is by doing it repeatedly
until it becomes your normal."

Okay, now that you know what's most important to citizens, so what? Well, if you are serious about continuously improving our profession by increasing citizen satisfaction, then a suitable place to start is developing the habit in those *"little matters"* Colin Powell referred to. And the most important *"little matter"* is what happens in the middle (the Process) of the encounter.

CHAPTER 4 EXCELLENCE KEYS

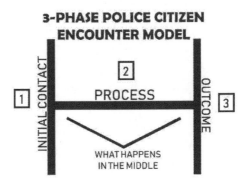

> ➤ 3 Phase Police-Citizen Encounter Model
> > ✓ Initial Contact
> > ✓ Process (what happens in the middle)
> > ✓ Outcome

> ➤ Citizens' satisfaction levels increase when they feel they are treated with a fundamental fairness on *how* you arrived at the outcome. Fairness trumps even perceived favorable outcomes for citizens.

> ➤ Sometimes the police are the ones that start off an encounter on the wrong foot, but they can make up for it during the process.

> ➤ Excellence demands more from us, it demands we be the adult in the room, regardless of the situation.

> ➤ The only way to develop a habit is by doing it repeatedly until it becomes *your* normal. Excellence in all you do is a habit.

CHAPTER 5

3 C's of Community Expectations

> "You are in the service industry, whether you choose to embrace it or not."

Successful business owners know their customers' needs and wants and then provide both. It's no different for us if we want to exceed citizen expectations and achieve more success. You are in the service industry, whether you choose to embrace that or not; hence the name, servants.

So, what do citizens really expect from you? Have you ever thought about that? One of my most challenging and enlightening assignments was serving as the chief spokesperson for my department in a top five television market. I will never forget one incident that occurred during my time there that made me think about this.

Our department was about to release a dash cam video that contained all the ingredients for a perfect media storm. The video contained a highly emotional situation, an NFL running back, and the police; it did not disappoint.

This incident involved a simple traffic stop. It was not a questionable officer involved shooting, excessive force caught on camera, or an officer berating a citizen; it was a traffic stop. But this traffic stop gained national attention. Perhaps you remember seeing it on the news or hearing about it. Here's the story.

A patrol officer observed a vehicle with its hazard lights on driving through a red light early one early morning during midnight shift. The officer turned his reds and blues on and proceeded to follow the vehicle into a hospital emergency room parking lot to conduct the stop. The initial stop seemed normal until the actual personal interaction began (the middle of the encounter). What the officer didn't know at the time was that the driver was rushing to the hospital for him and his wife to see their mother (and in-law), who was critically ill and on the verge of passing away. The driver's wife, understandably emotional, exited the vehicle in a rush to see her dying mother. The officer, not knowing what he had initially, ordered the driver to remain at the scene demanding to see identification and insurance paperwork. The driver became a bit frustrated with the officer because he was also wanting to see his mother-in-law. The driver told the officer the reason they were there several times to no avail.

The officer appeared unsympathetic of the driver's situation and seemed more concerned about handling the business part of the traffic stop. At the onset, the driver could not find his insurance paperwork. The longer the encounter continued, the more frustrated both parties became. Still, the officer stood his ground, demanding to see the appropriate documentation.

After several minutes of mounting frustration on both sides, an emergency room hospital nurse walked outside to inform the officer of the urgent situation. Another officer from a neighboring agency arrived and attempted to intervene as well. The patrol officer did not budge, continuing to threaten the driver with towing the vehicle and even an arrest. Unfortunately, the driver's mother-in-law died during the encounter.

Now, let's return to the releasing of the dash cam video to the media. Remember, this encounter began as a traffic stop. The news story along with the video aired during the local evening news, and that's when all hell broke loose. The following morning, my voicemail was full of citizens' messages that were outraged at what they had seen the night before on the news. Citizens were calling the police media office and all of our patrol substations to give us a piece of their minds! Our departmental leadership issued a statement on our website responding to the immense attention this story had gained. This was unprecedented. By this time other media outlets, including all the major national networks, also requested a copy of the video. We decided to hold a press conference that same afternoon so Police Chief David Kunkle could respond publicly. This was too big of a story for anyone else on the department to respond; it had to come from the top.

The chief publicly apologized to the family for their negative experience with one of our officers. "His behavior, in my opinion, did not exhibit the common sense, the discretion, the compassion that we expect our officers to exhibit," Kunkle told The Associated Press.[xiii] The Chief explained that poor judgment was used during this incident, and this was not representative of the police department's values. Even though the media kept this story alive for a few more days after the press conference, citizens' calls dwindled and eventually stopped altogether. It was as if the community breathed a sigh of relief when they heard the heartfelt message from the chief.

I believe that citizens recognized and felt the Chief's GETIT Factor. Citizens want to know that the police GET~IT; that the police get (understand) them. It's important that we (the police) never forget that we are first and foremost citizens. Wearing a uniform doesn't separate you from the community; it makes you more a part of it. This incident made me reflect on what the community really expects from the police and how this experience could be used as a teachable moment for all of us. Excellence requires us to do so.

"Wearing a uniform doesn't separate you from the
community; it makes you more a part of it."

Being a visual person, I pictured Ms. Smith sitting at home watching this news story for the first time in Anytown, USA. As Ms. Smith sees this story unfolding, she begins to process what she is witnessing to try and make sense of it. Ms. Smith begins to feel a bit uncomfortable, so the internal conflict begins. You see, Ms. Smith, like many citizens, supports the police and wants to give them the benefit of the doubt. On one hand, she is glad that someone else is the one conducting that traffic stop, especially at that time of the night. Ms. Smith recognizes how dangerous police work can be. On the other hand, she acknowledges that this family had an obvious sense of urgency.

The internal conflict began when the interaction between the driver and officer began. Can't you just see Ms. Smith paying close attention to both sides and trying to make sense of this as it is unfolding in front of her eyes for the first time? Her initial feeling is probably to trust that the police officer knows what he is doing, but after obvious signs of this being a legitimate family emergency, it becomes more and more difficult for Ms. Smith to comprehend. At some point during the interaction, Ms. Smith simply could not support the officer anymore. In her mind, the officer's actions had gone too far this time.

What happened to Ms. Smith? What was the breaking point when she finally thought, *This is too much already!* Ms. Smith, as many others did, placed herself in that same situation. Ms. Smith wondered, *"What if that was me rushing to see my mother for the last time and I didn't have the opportunity to do so, or what if those were my sons and daughters coming to see me in my final minutes and we missed the opportunity to see each other one final time?"* That's precisely what countless of people felt when they watched this encounter unfold.

They placed themselves there that night and they did not like what they observed and more than that, how they felt. The delegated authority (trust and consent) given to that officer had been misused.

Let's think about this a little more. I have no idea what the officer was thinking that night, only what his actions were. I am cognizant, however, that there were no winners. Let's not forget that this officer's career and life were also affected. From what I understand, this was a hard-working officer, always above average and often led his sector in activity. All it took was one negative encounter to cancel everything out. Fair or unfair, that is the reality of our chosen profession. Every encounter matters!

As I travel across the country speaking on Excellence in Policing with police from all ranks, the number one leadership challenge I hear repeatedly is the lack of engagement from first line supervisors with their troops. Leaders, are you doing enough to protect your officers from crossing that proverbial point of no return? Are you observing your officers in action? I'm not referring to only the 'hot calls' like shootings and such but calls and traffic stops where there is more personal citizen interaction. Are you reviewing citizen complaints that may show a pattern of behavior that can negatively impact your officer's career and life? In other words, do you care enough to do all of the above and more? I believe you do. Protecting your officers from physical harm and keeping their careers intact is your responsibility.

Here's one uncomplicated way to communicate citizen's expectations to your officers. I call it the 3 C's of Community Expectations:

1. COMPETENCE- citizens expect the police to know their job and do it well, especially if they are going to be taking people's freedom away. Fortunately, law enforcement does a pretty good job at training police officers the fundamentals of the job. Yes, mistakes are made

but overall, officers are proficient. However, learning must never cease so that an officer's competency is never questioned.

In the above scenario, citizens did not have a problem with the traffic stop itself. It was legitimate in their eyes. In fact, there may have been a different issue if the officer did not take any action. Most citizens understand the safety factor involved for officers during traffic stops. Citizens know people lie to you and as rare as it may be, that some may even drive into an emergency room parking lot to get out of a ticket!

2. COMPASSION - citizens do not want to deal with robots; they want to deal with real people! Human beings have feelings and even show them at times. This goes back to that GETIT Factor. The police should never forget to place themselves in the citizen's shoes and show them that you understand. I am not suggesting hugs for everyone or anything close to that. Let me just say it like this, don't be an asshole! Show people you care, because you do.

3. COMMON SENSE - yes, citizens would very much appreciate it if you used more common sense. Let's begin with defining common sense, according to Merriam-Webster: *the ability to think and behave in a reasonable way and to make good decisions.*[xiv]

"Let me just say it like this, don't be an asshole!"

Be reasonable! This means to be fair and to use good judgment. I am not completely certain if common sense can be taught. Heck, I've asked people to define common sense and most struggle with this. People know what it is and is not, it's just difficult to explain. Here's my crack at it- In policing, common sense is acknowledging that we all live in this same world and share many things. It means making decisions that are in the best interest of both yourself and those you encounter. Always consider others' feelings and circumstances by placing yourself in their situation and act how you would want an officer to treat you or one of your family members under the same circumstance.

Let this be your guide through every police-citizen encounter.

CHAPTER 5 EXCELLENCE KEYS

➤ You are in the service industry, whether you choose to embrace that or not.

➤ The GETIT Factor - citizens want to know that the police *GET IT*, that the police get (understand) them.

➤ 3 C's of Community Expectations

✓ COMPETENCE - citizens expect the police to know their job and do it well.

✓ COMPASSION - citizens don't want to speak to robots, they want you to be human! Human beings have feelings and even show them at times.

✓ COMMON SENSE - the ability to think and behave in a reasonable way and to make good decisions.

➤ Wearing a uniform doesn't separate you from the community; it makes you more part of it.

➤ In policing, common sense is acknowledging that we all live in this same world and share many things. It means making decisions that are in the best interest of both yourself and those you encounter.

➤ Don't be an asshole!

CHAPTER 6

AUTHORITY AND POWER

> "Authority is a gift from those we serve. What we do with it is our gift back to them."

Legitimate authority comes from the people; always has, always will. Part of the journey to Excellence in Policing is appreciating the difference between authority and power and recognizing its relevance to policing today, maybe more than ever. Both are necessary, and the police should always consider the appropriateness of when and how much to apply each of them.

Authority is delegated influence, the right to rule. Power, on the other hand, is strength or using physical force to accomplish something. Think of the word 'delegated' for a second. It means to give control, responsibility, and authority to someone; to entrust to another. It can also mean to send another as one's representative.[xv] Authority, delegated to the police by the people, is something the police should treat as sacred. Consider this- the public has placed their trust in you, to do the right thing and for the right reason on their behalf. You are their representative.

Here's an illustration and a commonly used example that shows the difference between authority and power. Picture a uniformed police officer standing in the middle of a street with her hand up toward an oncoming 18-wheeler. The driver (hopefully) will inevitably press his brakes until coming to a complete stop. The truck driver recognizes that the uniform with a badge symbolizes authority. In this scenario, the truck has power, but the police officer has authority. Authority is the reason the driver will comply by stopping the vehicle. Conversely, if that same officer attempts to use only power to stop the same 18-wheeler, well, you know what happens next. In this case, the 18-wheeler holds the power. There's a significant difference between authority and power. But in policing, both are necessary to maintain social order, manage conflict, and solve problems in the community.

Using power without authority is a dangerous place to be. Imagine having to use physical force, or power, without legitimate authority (in the eyes of the public) to diffuse a situation or even protect a human life. Society is demanding that the police use less power; and this is a good thing for all, especially for the police. Therefore, the police should rely on using their authority more. One of the ways to increase our influence (authority) is to practice procedural justice (covered in Chapter 8). Procedural justice leads to increased police legitimacy (Chapter 7), which leads to increased authority.

> "Using power without authority is a dangerous place to be."

Authority and power go hand in hand in policing, not separate from each other. However, without trust, there is no authority. Without authority, policing becomes much more dangerous. The two types of authority, legal and legitimate, are covered in the next chapter. The police should never take their delegated authority for granted. Think of authority like this- *"Authority is a gift from those you serve. What you do with it is your gift back to them."*

CHAPTER 6 EXCELLENCE KEYS

➤ Legitimate police authority comes from the people.

➤ Authority is delegated influence, the right to rule.

➤ Power is strength or using physical force to accomplish something.

➤ Authority and Power are necessary to maintain social order, manage conflict, and solve problems in the community.

➤ Power without authority is a dangerous place to be.

➤ Society is demanding that the police use less power; and this is a good thing for all, especially for the police.

➤ Authority is a gift from those you serve. What you do with it is your gift back to them.

CHAPTER 7

THE CORNERSTONES OF POLICING: TRUST AND LEGITIMACY

If you are going to be Excellent, then staying informed of current literature regarding our profession is essential. In May 2015, the Final Report of the President's Task Force on 21st Century Policing was released.[xvi] This report was created as a blueprint to help policing move forward. It's not only about surviving the adversity police face today but thriving in the midst of it. I strongly encourage you to read the report in its entirety here:

https://cops.usdoj.gov/pdf/taskforce/TaskForce_FinalReport.pdf

These next couple of chapters will be a slightly academic portion of the book. Stay with me though, it may be the most important part. As leaders, we should always be challenging our belief systems. The best way to do this is by reading more, considering what academia offers policing, and thinking critically about issues.

The very first 'pillar' of 21st Century Policing is Building Trust and Legitimacy. It is vital for the police to understand the concept of police legitimacy and its importance to building and maintaining community trust. Police legitimacy reflects the belief that the police ought to be allowed to exercise their authority to maintain social order, manage conflicts, and solve problems in their communities.[xvii] Reflect on this for a moment, "the police ought to be allowed to exercise their authority…" When your citizens view you as legitimate, they not only expect and want you to exercise your authority, but they are cheering you on! Legitimacy is such a powerful tool for the police that they should be doing everything in their control to maintain and increase it. The more citizens view or perceive the police as legitimate, the more authority the police will have to do their job more effectively. Authority reflects delegated influence and as you know, leadership is influence. People with high leadership skills (influence) have followers who would charge the hill with him/her. Apply this concept to policing, and your ability to do those things the community expects from you becomes easier. Citizens want you to succeed, they know if we're successful, communities are safer and their quality of life increases. This is a win-win.

There are two types of authority that are worth discussing. First, there is *legitimate authority* and much like respect, this type is earned. It's what gives you more influence. Legitimacy and trust is largely based on citizens' perception that the police have their best interest in mind.[xviii] So what does having "their best interest in mind" mean exactly? Well, it's time to get real here. Officers, understandably so, are trained to cover their asses (CYA) in everything they do. You've heard these many times. This is so the police can protect their livelihood to provide for their families, it's a must! There is obviously nothing wrong with protecting your families. However, it's when officers solely act out of their own best interest when making decisions and enforcing laws that can clash with building trust and legitimacy with its citizenry.

> "The police should always act in the best interest of both the community and the police when making decisions and taking action."

These two 'competing interests' can present a conflict when officers are *only* seeking self-gain or career survival. The police should always act in the best interest of both the community and the police when making decisions and taking action. The police should want what their citizens want (remember common sense). Do you want to live in a safe neighborhood? Do you want and expect other officers to have your best interest in mind if you ever must deal with them off duty? How would you feel if another officer cited you or a family member (preferably one that you like) with multiple violations because it was easy activity for them and nothing else? I can't see where that helps build public confidence and trust in the police.

The word community can be broken down into two words, *common* and *unity*. The things we have in common are what unite us-*Community!* Again, wearing a uniform doesn't separate you from the community; it makes you more a part of it. In front of the book I included Sir Robert Peel's 9 Principles as a reminder of why the police were created. These principles should still hold true today. And while community, this principle applies, … "the police are the public and the public are the police." We are one.

"Wearing a uniform doesn't separate you from the community; it makes you more a part of it."

When making decisions, a simple question to ask yourself is, "How will my actions impact the community as a whole?" Most of the time your actions will benefit the community, whether it's arresting a drunk driver or issuing a hazardous driving violation citation. Heck, even something as minor as issuing a parking citation can be in the best interest of the community. Most people can understand and support your actions when it's for the greater good. It's when officers go out of their way to build up their activity or perhaps take unnecessary action out of pure boredom that citizens become frustrated and begin to question officers' true intentions. This is where the argument can be made about quality versus quantity. If you are serious about building trust, then it's important that officers take the right actions for the right reasons.

The other type of authority is *legal authority*. This is the formal authority the police derive from the Constitution and state and local statutes.[xix] The problem with relying solely on legal authority is that life doesn't always fit perfectly into rules or laws. This is where police officers that see only in black and white get into trouble. Life demands us to know how to effectively operate in the grey area. Common sense and good judgement must prevail to make the best decision in the best interest of both the police and the community.

"...life doesn't always fit into rules or laws."

Relying only on legal authority may work short term but will ultimately be counter-productive. If police organizations display an 'us against them' attitude or a 'we know what's best for them' approach, then this can lead to a loss in public confidence and trust. To prevent this from happening, the police will need to have a clearer grasp of what the community needs and expects from them.

Professor Dennis Rosenbaum pointed out that "residents will insist on aggressive policing and enforcement up to the point where it directly affects them, their family, or their friends, who frequently end up in jail or report being mistreated by police."[xx]   For example, zero tolerance enforcement should be used sparingly and with precision; using only *legal authority* may yield an unintended consequence of negatively perceived treatment by the police.   Communities, particularly high crime areas (hot spots), should be able "to experience both safety and liberty and not be required to choose one or the other."[xxi]   If we discount how the community perceives their police department, then meaningful impact will be difficult to achieve.

There is an enormous difference between legitimate and legal authority. When we rely more on and use legitimate authority, people will more voluntarily comply and work with the police. And, hopefully give you the benefit of the doubt more so than not. In today's social media world, having benefit of the doubt when something that may even hint at being controversial occurs in your city is a powerful advantage to have. Heck, not too long ago, it at least took a minute or two for a video to be uploaded and shared to the world. Now with Facebook Live, it's real time! What a crazy world we live in these days. It used to be that police leaders had the luxury of responding to an incident when they were ready. Those days are long gone. Consider this, wouldn't it be great if your residents gave you the benefit of the doubt, at least initially, so your department can provide the facts and respond accordingly? This requires an elevated level of trust between the community and your police department.

Building trust is not solely about attending community events and speaking at crime watches, although these are important. Trust comes from, largely in part, the way the public perceives you based on how they are treated. Making deposits in that proverbial trust account should be continuous. It will be too late if you're in the red when something happens in your city. It is important that you and every officer in your department are constantly depositing trust during every police citizen encounter! Remember, every citizen encounter is a commercial for your department. Our profits will be measured by the amount of confidence and trust our citizens have in us.

Here's another question. Have you ever wondered why most people obey the law and why this may be important to our success? Many people obey the law because they feel the authorities enforcing them have the right to dictate behavior.[xxii] Sure, consequences of a fine and/or jail time can be a crime deterrent. However, if the police solely were to depend on that to impact crime, they are going to fall short. Again, thank God that most people believe obeying the law is the right thing to do. Most people have intrinsic values that guide them in the right direction. They don't always get it right- heck, who does, but citizens with these values help the police in many ways including combating crime. Therefore, building legitimacy helps the police succeed!

Imagine how difficult it would be to perform your duties as a police officer if the public did not see you as a legitimate authority? It wouldn't be difficult; it would be impossible. Policing would become even more dangerous. Maintaining and building police legitimacy is vital to our success. The more legitimacy the police have, the stronger and safer you and your communities will be.

CHAPTER 7 EXCELLENCE KEYS

➢ Legitimacy reflects the belief that the police ought to be allowed to exercise their authority to maintain social order, manage conflicts and solve problems in their communities.[xiii]

➢ Legitimacy and trust is largely based on citizens' perception that the police have their best interest in mind.[xiv]

➢ Legitimate authority, much like respect, is earned; this is what gives you influence.

➢ Officers solely acting solely out of their own best interest when making decisions can clash with building trust and legitimacy with its citizenry.

➢ The word community can be broken down into two words; common and unity. The things we have in common are what unite us- Community!

➢ The problem with relying solely on legal authority is that life doesn't always fit into rules or laws.

➢ Most people obey the law because they see authorities and laws as legitimate. Therefore, building legitimacy helps the police succeed.

CHAPTER 8

BUILDING LEGITIMACY THROUGH PROCEDURAL JUSTICE

"We must build a new world, a far better world - one in which the eternal dignity of man is respected." Harry S. Truman

Now that we've covered the concept of police legitimacy and why having it is important to policing, let's move on to how the police can increase it. One of the ways to achieve legitimacy is by practicing procedural justice during every police-citizen encounter. Procedural justice is a sociological term that has become relevant in the last few years as it relates to our profession. Tom Tyler and Tracy Meares are researchers who have studied procedural justice and legitimacy and brought it to the forefront of our profession. Again, if we are to remain excellent, then staying informed is one way of ensuring we do. I encourage you to learn more about their extraordinary work in these areas.

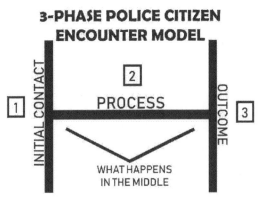

So, let's return to the 3-phase model for a second; the Initial

Contact, the Process (what happens in the middle), and the Outcome. In this chapter, we will focus primarily on the Process. Remember that most people are more concerned with the Process, even more than the Outcome, whether favorable or not. Procedural justice is the procedures (or actions) used by police officers where citizens are treated fairly and with proper respect as human beings.[xxiii] When citizens feel they are treated with dignity, respect, and fairness, their attitudes toward the police are more positive. These attitudes result in increased levels of trust and confidence in us. Conversely, increased levels of trust will result in increased legitimacy. The more trust and confidence citizens have in the police, the more willing they will be to work with us and comply with our demands. In contrast, "...positive attitudes about the police drop when citizens feel that they have been treated unfairly, disrespected, not listened to, or physically abused during encounters with the police."[xxiv] This is why procedural justice should be the foundation of every police-citizen encounter. Procedural justice leads to increased legitimacy, and that's the goal.

Crime fighting is and will always be part of policing. Police officers still cannot fight crime independently and be effective, at least not long term. This responsibility should be shared with the community. Without trust and confidence in the police, it will be difficult to be true partners in combating crime, if not impossible. Without trust, the consequences are enormous and range from lawsuits to a declining willingness to obey the law.[xxv] Simply put, the police cannot afford not to be legitimate in the eyes of its citizens.

Tom Tyler breaks down procedural justice into two parts and four tenets. These tenets should be practiced throughout the entirety of any encounter, but most certainly during the middle (the Process). Again, people are more concerned about the Process- even more than the Outcome.

The first part is how the officer makes his/her decision. It's important for people to tell their side of the story. Everyone wants to be heard. The first tenet is *Voice-* this includes both listening and explaining. Following these tenets will help you better manage perception as well. Allow the citizen to tell their story, even if you choose not to take their side when deciding. Be genuinely interested in what the citizen has to say. This makes people feel more a part of the Process and perhaps feel a bit more in control of a perceived fairer Outcome. Being able to share their side certainly helps with the fairness issue. In turn, taking the time to explain the reason you're standing in front of them in the first place, your intended action, and the reasoning behind it adds a sense of openness and respect towards that individual.

Tyler's second tenet is *Neutrality-* whether the officer appears neutral and unbiased. This is where the concept of managing perception is crucial. While I strongly believe that most officers are doing the right things for the right reasons, I've also learned that an officer failing to manage perception can result in a misunderstanding or a feeling of the officer not being neutral. Ultimately, these feelings can turn into complaints. And now that ball begins to roll, and you know what happens next.

Police must play chess and not checkers; managing perception will always be a power move. Citizens are more informed today and extremely interested in your every move. Increased citizens' awareness is a good thing. However, the onus is on you (the police) to manage perception as best as you can.

> "Police must play chess and not checkers; managing perception will always be a power move."

I like to tell this story of what failing to manage perception may look like out on patrol.

Two patrol officers arrive at a residence regarding a suspicious person call. The resident walks outside to speak with the officers and proceeds to tell them a young man wearing a black shirt, jean shorts, and carrying a backpack was walking through the neighborhood and appeared to be up to no good. The neighborhood was recently hit hard by burglaries, and the police have been pleading with the residents to call 911 if they see or hear anything suspicious. So, this resident finally obliges and calls the police. The resident informs to tell the responding officers that the young man was last seen walking eastbound on her street a short while ago. All the officers say is thank you, then make a U-turn and drive westbound. The caller observes their actions and probably wonders, "Why in the hell did I call 911? The officers did the exact opposite of what I just told them!" What actually occurred was that the officers, knowing their beat well, were quite confident that the suspect was Johnny, and he usually hangs out at the C Store which is located just west of the location. That's why the officers made that U-turn. But because the officers failed to manage perception by choosing not to take a few seconds to explain their actions, the resident felt this was a waste of her time, and her confidence level on the police probably decreased. All the officers had to do is state they were confident they knew the suspect and would be driving straight to where he is known to hang out.

Officers should, when feasible and safe, take the time to share what they're going to do next. If the officers in the above scenario would have done this, the resident would have felt validated and probably continued to call the police in the future. In addition, the resident's potential feelings of resentment and frustration could have been avoided.

Tyler's second part of procedural justice is the quality of treatment throughout the encounter. This part includes the third tenet-*Respect*. Respect is to hold in high regard because of their value.[xxvi] All citizens want and deserve to be treated with respect. You and I are no different.

There are simple ways to show respect. One way is by doing what we already covered-*listen*. Take it one step further by actively listening. Make sure and maintain eye contact with the citizen. This shows the citizen they have your undivided attention and that you are interested in what they have to say. Acknowledge what the citizen told you by saying something like, "I can understand rushing to get the kids off to school on time. I am a parent, I get it. However, the last thing anyone wants is for you and your beautiful children to be harmed in any way. Please slow down."

Be helpful. Always find ways to help. Whether it's by providing a citizen with a phone number or address to another city department or giving them directions to an event in your city, help them! People will appreciate that more than you think. Refer to your citizens by their titles like Sir, Ma'am, Dr., Pastor, Father- whatever. And always thank the citizen when appropriate. A simple, "Thank you" goes a long way in showing respect. I know, these are super simple things to do and most of you are already doing these and more. But if you can improve in any one of these, you're being excellent!

Consider how you would like to be treated by an officer on a traffic stop, or take it further-how would you expect your wife, son, or daughter be treated if they encountered an officer? Have you ever been pulled over by an officer and felt minimized or disrespected? Remember how that felt? And that's because you're an officer who can relate; imagine how a citizen may feel.

The fourth and final principle includes whether the officer appears-*Trustworthy*. Does the citizen feel as if they are being treated in a fair and transparent manner? In other words, are the officers open about what and, perhaps more importantly, about *why* they are taking certain actions? Be open about what you're doing. Heck, you're doing the right thing anyway so don't be hesitant to show it. Plus, this also helps manage perception.

It's important that officers not give the impression that they may be hiding something from the citizen. Also, your body language, specifically your facial expressions, may make you appear more trustworthy. One study in the journal Personality and Social Psychology Bulletin found that "the slightly happier a person appeared, the more likely he was rated to be trustworthy."[xxvii] I strongly suggest that you show citizens that you're human by not being so robotic all the time. Be human! If research shows that happier faces seem more trustworthy, then it's in your best interest to crack that smile more often when it's appropriate. Don't overdo it though; people will think you're just weird.

Amid what some may say is a no-win battle for the police, increasing legitimacy by practicing procedural justice can lead to more positive results and a higher level of satisfaction in our profession. Studies suggest these results include the following: greater public deference to the police when the police have personal interactions with members of the community, increased compliance with the law, higher levels of cooperation with police efforts to manage crime, and stronger institutional support for police departments.[xxviii] The real question is, "Why wouldn't you want to practice procedural justice?"

There is no doubt that both police officers and citizens benefit from practicing procedural justice. The main question is whether YOU will strive for Excellence in Policing by taking the first step in treating others with dignity and respect. If you're waiting for others to do it first, good luck with that. I often hear people say things like, "When they change, I will change." Well, I will just tell you that "they" does not exist. "They" is a figment of your imagination. In reality, "they" is you. YOU will have to take the first step. As painful as it may be at times, the return on your investment will pay huge dividends. You and your officers will be safer, experience less stress, positively impact crime, and increase mutual respect and understanding. All these benefits will be covered in the next chapter.

CHAPTER 8 EXCELLENCE KEYS

> One of the ways to achieve legitimacy is by practicing procedural justice in every police-citizen encounter.

> Procedural justice is the procedures (or actions) used by police officers where citizens are treated fairly and with proper respect as human beings

> When citizens feel they are treated with dignity, respect, and fairness, their attitudes toward the police are more positive.

> Tom Tyler breaks down procedural justice into two parts and four tenets.

1. How an Officer makes his/her decision

    a. *Voice* - Explain your actions - allow citizen to tell their side of the story and genuinely listen to their side.

    b. *Neutrality*- Does the citizen feel the officer was neutral and unbiased?

2. Quality of treatment throughout the encounter

    a. *Respect* - show citizens respect

    b. *Trustworthy* - Does the citizen feel as if they are being treated in a fair and transparent manner?

> Citizens are more informed today and extremely interested in your every move. This is a good thing; however, it places the onus on you more so to manage perception the very best you can.

CHAPTER 9

A CASE FOR PROCEDURAL JUSTICE

SAFETY

Practicing procedural justice is good business for police officers. Safety is always most important, for both you and those you encounter. So, let's begin here. We now know that when people feel they are treated with a level of dignity and respect, often, they will voluntarily comply with your requests and demands. The more citizens comply because of your legitimate authority (delegated influence), the less you will have to use force or power. This lessens the chance for you to get hurt. Let's face it; when the police must use force, officers get injured. You've probably seen it and/or endured broken fingers, twisted ankles, knee sprains, and the list goes on. You can lessen the *getting injured* part by practicing procedural justice. Besides, you can't help anyone (fellow officers and citizens) sitting at home or working the station passing out radios because you're hurt. Most important, your family needs you to stay healthy. Who can argue against that?

STRESS

Police officers deal with stress every day. According to a recent Forbes article, The 10 Most Stressful Jobs In 2016, police officers were listed #4. Officers' average life spans are around 66 years of age, about 10 years lower than the average male in the United States.[xxix] This alone should be enough to motivate you to lower your stress level. The pink elephant in the room for police officers is the issue of suicide. No one feels comfortable talking about that. But if you've been in law enforcement for any amount of time, you've been affected by this tragedy. Fortunately, we are seeing more and more awareness and training being offered in this area. I do believe that less stress can help with this genuine issue as well. We all need to enjoy our lives more. There is so much to look forward to like retirement, travel, and grandkids. Enough said.

One of the most stressful aspects of being in law enforcement is having to deal with citizen complaints, even when the officer knows he didn't do anything wrong. By the way, rudeness is the number one complaint across the board in every department. You know the deal - the citizen calls the station to complain about you, and next thing you know, your sergeant is calling over the radio directing you to head to the station. You begin mentally scrolling through the events of the day to think of what you may have done wrong. You ask yourself, "Did I piss someone off?" What happens next? Your heart rate and blood pressure increase as you drive to the station. There is something about when your sergeant/supervisor wants to speak with you that causes stress.

Anytime there is a violation of trust from the citizen's perspective, it could result in a complaint. It may be something an officer may consider of little significance such as not allowing the citizen to tell their side of the story, the officer's tone was 'harsh', or the citizen feeling that she was not treated fairly. These are all examples of citizen complaints that can be avoided by practicing procedural justice during every encounter.

IMPACT CRIME

"Play chess by empowering your community by partnering with them to be a force multiplier for your department."

Let's never forget that the police are first and foremost crime fighters. Your communities still expect you to deal with crime and maintain social order. Here's the thing though, treating people fairly and with dignity and respect (procedural justice) will also positively impact crime. Consider this, the more citizens trust and feel confident about their police department, the more likely they will be to cooperate with officers. Increased cooperation means more information sharing, more witnesses willing to come forward about crimes, and an increased shared responsibility for preventing crime.

Reducing crime long term will never be achieved using strict law enforcement tactics, a zero-tolerance approach, or a 'we know what's best for you' mentality. It has always been the case that the police cannot combat crime alone. We will always need the public's help. Play chess by empowering your community by partnering with them to be a force multiplier for your department. This is good business.

CHAPTER 9 EXCELLENCE KEYS

> The more citizens comply because of your legitimate authority (remember delegated influence), the less you will have to use force or power.

> Most citizen complaints can be avoided by practicing procedural justice during every encounter.

> Play chess by empowering your community by partnering with them to be a force multiplier for your department.

> Practicing procedural justice will make you and your officers safer, experience less stress, and positively impact crime.

CHAPTER 10

A CASE FOR BUILDING MUTUAL RESPECT AND UNDERSTANDING

Perhaps the greatest challenge for both officers and citizens is increasing both mutual respect and understanding. I believe one way is to exercise procedural justice during every police-citizen encounter. The adage about first giving respect to earn respect is true. If officers expect citizens to show them respect, we will have to show it first. No disrespect to anyone, but someone must be the adult in the room; tag, you're it. The community expects YOU to be the adult in the room.

One of the conflicts officers face when dealing with the public is when citizens believe they really understand your job. We both know that the reality is that they don't! One of the procedural justice tenets is explaining what and, more importantly, *why* an officer acted. When an officer takes the time to explain, the citizen can more clearly understand his/her actions and accept them as a result. Additionally, this increases their understanding of what it is you do. Doing this also helps minimize citizen complaints. Again, win-win.

If the police seek first to understand, one of Stephen Covey's *7 Habits of Highly Successful People*, then the police must first acknowledge that citizens already have a preconception about you. Seeking first to understand can result in effectively managing perception and avoiding pitfalls that can lead to citizen dissatisfaction or decreased confidence and trust in the police.

It happens all too often- the police and citizens' worlds collide. Again, one of the challenges for the police is that many citizens believe they really know the job of a police officer. You may have heard it referred to as the CSI effect. Whatever you want to call it, their beliefs usually contradict the realities of policing. A good example of this was an incident that occurred in Cambridge, Massachusetts that gained national attention involving a veteran Cambridge Police Department Sergeant and a well-known Harvard Professor. You probably remember the infamous beer summit at the White House with President Obama shortly after these two worlds collided in Cambridge. The goal for the meeting was to gain a clearer understanding of each other's world. Whether or not that was accomplished, I don't know, but at least they tried.

The significance of this incident is that this could have occurred in Any Town, USA. In fact, this is reflective of encounters that occur between police officers and citizens every day at some level. This incident just happened to gain national attention. I appreciate Cambridge Police Commissioner Robert C. Haas for having the courage to allow this incident to be dissected as well as Sgt. Crowley and Professor Gates for sharing their experiences for the betterment of policing. It's important to emphasize that the intent of this chapter is not to criticize either party, but rather to learn from this teachable moment.

For this chapter, I want to focus primarily on the differing accounts of what occurred that day to illustrate how increasing mutual respect and understanding can help manage police-citizen encounters. You will be surprised at just how different Sgt. Crowley and Professor Gates' perspectives were regarding the exact same incident. Here are both versions of what occurred during their encounter. These were taken directly from the Cambridge Review Committee's (CRC) final report titled *Missed Opportunities, Shared Responsibilities: Final Report of the Cambridge Review Committee.* I strongly encourage you to read the entire case study at

http://www2.cambridgema.gov/CityOfCambridge_Content/documents/C ambridge%20Review_FINAL.pdf

THE 911 CALL

On July 16th, 2009, The Cambridge Emergency Communications Center (ECC), the city's 911 center, received a call at 12:43 p.m. According to the caller, an elderly woman had observed two men with suitcases attempting to enter a residence on Ware Street in Cambridge. The elderly woman expressed concern to the caller that the men were attempting to break into someone's home. The caller observed that the front door screen had been broken but expressed uncertainty about whether the men perhaps lived there and "just had a hard time with a key." At 12:46 p.m., a Cambridge Police patrol unit in the area was dispatched to respond to Ware Street for a "possible breaking and entering in progress."

Sergeant James Crowley radioed that he would respond, since he was nearby on Harvard Street. After arriving at the scene, Sergeant Crowley requested that the department "keep the cars coming."

ACCORDING TO SERGEANT JAMES CROWLEY

Sergeant Crowley has a reputation for being a no-nonsense, by-the-book police officer. He has been commended for dedication and professional conduct for helping a diabetic victim avert a tragedy and for diligence that resulted in an arrest and successful investigative case closure. Among his peers, regardless of their race, Crowley is well liked and respected on the force. In 1993, Crowley was a campus police officer at Brandeis University when he administered CPR trying to save the life of former Boston Celtics player Reggie Lewis. He was selected by former Police Commissioner Ronnie Watson to teach a class on preventing racial profiling at the Police Academy in Lowell, Mass. He has conducted that training, along with an African-American officer, for five years.

During the past five years, Sergeant Crowley has made 12 arrests, including one arrest of a disorderly person, one for disturbing the peace, and three for unlawful assembly. It is important to understand that sergeants, with multiple and varied supervisory and administrative duties, including guiding officers in arrest situations, do not normally make large numbers of arrests themselves.

Sergeant Crowley reported that he arrived at the Ware Street residence in full uniform, with his nametag and badge number clearly displayed, as required by the Police Department. The recording of the 911 call shows that the caller said she was "not really sure" about the race of the men attempting to enter the residence, but that "one looked kind of Hispanic."

But according to Crowley's Incident Report, by the time he arrived and spoke to the 911 caller on the sidewalk in front of the house, she told him that she had observed "what appeared to be two black males" on the porch. Crowley stated that the caller said she was suspicious because she saw one of the men wedging his shoulder into the door, as if he were trying to force entry.

In his Incident Report, Crowley reported that "since I was the only police officer on location and had my back to the front door," he asked the caller to wait for other responding officers while he investigated further. Crowley reported to the Committee that he walked onto Professor Gates' front porch and felt very exposed because of the large windows he had to pass by. He looked into the home and saw an older black man in the foyer, whom Crowley, motioning with his hand, asked to step out onto the porch. According to Crowley, the man, who later identified himself as Henry Louis Gates, Jr., refused, saying, "No, I will not." Crowley claimed that Gates demanded to know who Crowley was, and Crowley said he identified himself as "Sergeant Crowley from the Cambridge Police" and informed Gates that he was there to investigate a report of a break-in in progress at the residence. Crowley reports that it was at this point that Gates opened his door and exclaimed, "Why, because I am a black man in America?" Crowley stated that he then asked Gates if there was anyone else in the house, to which Gates yelled that it was none of his business. Crowley said that Professor Gates then accused Crowley of being a racist police officer.

Crowley said he assured Gates that he was responding to a citizen's call to the Cambridge Police Department and the caller was still present, outside. Crowley said Gates then telephoned an unknown person and asked that person to "get the chief," and then told whoever was on the line that he was dealing with a racist police officer. According to Crowley, Gates then told Crowley he had no idea who he was "messing" with and that he hadn't heard the last of this.

At this point in his Incident Report account, Crowley wrote, "While I was led to believe that Gates was lawfully in the residence, I was quite surprised and confused with the behavior he exhibited toward me." Crowley said he then asked Gates for photo identification so he could verify that Gates, in fact, resided there. Crowley said Gates refused initially but later complied, showing a Harvard identification card. Crowley reported that upon learning that Gates was affiliated with Harvard, he radioed ECC and requested the presence of the Harvard University Police, and then prepared to leave the premises.

Crowley reported that Gates again demanded to know Crowley's name, accused Crowley of being a racist police officer, and said that he, Gates, "wasn't someone to mess with." Crowley became aware that Officer Carlos Figueroa was present. Crowley said that Gates continued to request his name and badge number. Crowley said that he told Gates that he had already provided his name twice upon Gates' request, that he was leaving Gates' residence, and that if he had any other questions, he "would speak to him outside of the residence." Crowley said that "my reason for wanting to leave the residence was that Gates was yelling very loud and the acoustics of the kitchen and foyer were making it difficult for me to transmit pertinent information to ECC or other responding units."

According to Crowley, he walked outside and noticed "several Cambridge and Harvard University police officers assembled on the sidewalk," as well as the 911 caller and at least seven passers-by looking in the direction of Gates, who had followed Crowley outside. Crowley's account in his police report stated that Gates was continuing to yell and behave in a "tumultuous" manner. Crowley stated that he warned Gates that he was becoming disorderly, but that

Gates ignored his warning and continued yelling, which caused the bystanders to appear "surprised and alarmed." Crowley said he warned Gates a second time while taking out his handcuffs, but that Gates again ignored his warning. Crowley then placed Gates under arrest.

Crowley reported that Gates objected to being handcuffed behind his back, because he said he was disabled and could not walk without a cane. Crowley ordered another officer to handcuff Gates with his hands in front and went into the house to retrieve Gates' cane. Crowley reported asking Gates if he wanted the property secured, to which Gates replied that the lock on the door was broken from a previous break-in attempt. A Harvard University maintenance person then arrived to secure the house.

Crowley's Incident Report states that Gates was arrested for disorderly conduct because he exhibited "loud and tumultuous behavior, in a public place, directed at a uniformed police officer who was present investigating a report of a crime in progress."

Five days later, the Middlesex County District Attorney's Office dropped the charge against Gates. The City of Cambridge, the Cambridge Police Department, and Professor Gates released a joint statement saying that "the incident of July 16th, 2009 was regrettable and unfortunate," and that dropping the charge was " a just resolution to an unfortunate set of circumstances."

ACCORDING TO PROFESSOR HENRY LOUIS GATES

Professor Gates is an American literary critic, educator, scholar, and writer. Professor Gates earned his M.A. and Ph.D. in English literature from Clare College at the University of Cambridge and his B.A. in history from Yale University, where he was a Scholar of the House. Professor Gates is currently the Alphonse Fletcher University Professor at Harvard University, where he is Director of the W.E.B. Du Bois Institute for African and African-American Research. Gates has previously taught at Yale, Cornell, and Duke Universities. Among his many other notable accomplishments, Gates was listed in Time as one of 1997's "25 Most Influential Americans." In January 2008, Gates co-founded The Root, a website dedicated to African-American perspectives, published by The Washington Post Company. Gates also serves on the boards of many institutions, including the New York Public Library, the Aspen Institute, the Brookings Institution, the NAACP Legal Defense Fund, the Harlem Educational Activities Fund, and the Center for Advanced Study in the Behavioral Sciences located in Stanford, California.

According to published reports and Professor Gates' interview with the Cambridge Review Committee, he was arriving home from the airport on July 16th, 2009. A local limousine company dropped Gates off at his home. Gates attempted to enter through the front door of the property but had trouble because the door was damaged. Specifically, Gates reported seeing damage suggesting that someone had tried to jimmy the lock; he also noticed a large footprint on the door. The limousine driver, whom Gates referred to as Driss, assisted Gates in attempting to gain entry to the house. Gates ultimately entered the rear entrance with his key and attempted to open the front door from the inside.

Gates was able, with the driver's help, to force the front door open and proceed through with his luggage.

The driver said that he noticed an elderly female looking at them from next door as they were trying to enter the house. Gates recalled Driss's comment at the time that the woman "was calling the police on us."

Gates reported that he called the Harvard Real Estate office to report the damage; while he was on the phone, he noticed a uniformed police officer on his front porch. Gates opened the door, and the officer asked Gates to step outside. Gates said that the officer's tone of voice made the hairs on the back of his neck stand up, and he refused to step outside.

Gates said he told the officer that he lived there and was a faculty member at Harvard University, and that the officer then asked him for proof that he lived there. Gates said he went into his kitchen, followed by Crowley, to get his wallet, and then placed his open wallet showing his Harvard identification card and Massachusetts driver's license on the counter for Crowley to see. Gates said that Officer Crowley did not respond. Gates said he asked for the officer's name and badge number on several occasions, but that the officer never responded or asked him if he was all right. Gates said that "the silence was deafening." Gates said he then said to the officer, "You're not responding because I am a black man and you're a white officer."

Gates said that Crowley said, "We are done here," and turned to leave the house. Gates then followed Crowley toward the front door, where he saw other police officers outside. When the officer left his home, Gates followed, still trying to get Crowley's badge number and name. Gates reported that as he again asked for the officer's identification, pointing his finger at Crowley's chest, the officer responded, "Thank you for accommodating my earlier request; now you're under arrest," and then placed Gates under arrest. Gates was then transported to the Cambridge Police Station and was held for four hours.

Gates told the Cambridge Review Committee that in retrospect, he would not have done anything differently, other than stepping outside onto the front porch after the encounter with Crowley inside the house. Gates said he could not understand why Crowley did not further explain why he had come to the house, but rather had remained silent. He said that during his encounter with Crowley, he became concerned that he was considered a suspect, because Crowley was not responding to his questions and seemed to take a long time studying his identification cards. He said he could not understand how Sergeant Crowley could think he was a burglar—a slight, elderly man who walks with a cane and who comes to the front door, telephone in hand, to talk to the police. "What criminal would do that?" he wondered.

CAMBRIDGE REVIEW COMMITTEE'S FINDINGS

This incident was avoidable.[xxx] The CRC found that both Sgt. Crowley and Professor Gates missed opportunities to deescalate the situation. The committee focused on misunderstandings, failed communications, and fear between the two men. While Sgt. Crowley was right about being cautious of a potentially dangerous encounter, once the threat was diminished, he should have taken steps to deescalate the situation. On the other hand, Professor Gates should have complied with Sgt. Crowley's demands and should have tried to understand the situation from a police officer's point of view. A measure of respect may have helped deescalate the circumstances. Sgt. Crowley felt he "had no choice" but to arrest the professor. However, the CRC believed there could have been a better outcome. Perhaps Sgt. Crowley should have taken "greater pains" to explain the uncertainty and potential dangers of the call; additionally, his duty to assess the risks may have caused him to "adopt a seemingly abrupt tone." [xxxi]

The CRC made it clear that the arrest of Professor Gates is not being questioned and noted that it was not unjustified. The point they did raise, however, is whether some police actions that may be "within policy" are not necessarily the best outcomes to a situation and may undermine the relationship between the police and the communities they serve.[xxxii]

A FEW THOUGHTS

So there you have it, same incident and two entirely different worlds. Both parties believed they were correct in how they handled the situation. In their interviews to the Cambridge Review Committee, each recalled "a level of confusion at each other's behavior." [xxxiii] Sgt. Crowley and Professor Gates never seemed to try to comprehend each other's perspective. The sergeant's primary concern was that of safety and possibly catching a burglar; the professor's apprehension was that he was being treated like a suspect rather than a law-abiding citizen.

73

Professor Gates interpreted Sgt. Crowley's actions, particularly his refusal to formally give his name and badge number, as an insult and an abuse of power.[xxxiv] Potentially dangerous encounters dictate that procedural justice be applied after a threat is diminished. Taking the time to explain why you took certain actions at the end can be just as effective as if it were done in the middle of the encounter (remember the Process).

Crowley stated he did, in fact, attempt to provide that information to Gates, but he was unable to do so because Gates was yelling so loudly. Crowley interpreted Gates' repeated questions as an attempt to be belligerent. Clearly, both parties did not seek first to understand, and the two worlds remained apart. Just because you can do something legally, doesn't mean it's necessary. As far as I know, there are no P.O.P (pissed off the police) laws in any penal code. I've looked, trust me. Listen, we all get it, some people must go to jail. We really do deal with straight up assholes out there. Therefore, most people couldn't and/or wouldn't do your job. They'd strongly prefer not to have to deal with any of that.

Even so, the police must be better than that. P.O.P arrests will get you in trouble and possibly cost you a lengthy career. Furthermore, P.O.P arrests go against everything we are trying to do in building trust, mutual respect, and mutual understanding. Playing chess requires us to use discretion wisely. If you're the only victim, except for physical harm of course, then solving that problem with solutions other than an arrest may be best for you. We must police smarter today.

During any encounter ask yourself, *"What do I want the result to look like?" "What is the win?"* This requires you to think and look 2 or 3 moves ahead (chess moves) to make better decisions now.

Discretion is our greatest tool *and* our greatest liability. We must protect having this tool by using it appropriately. The United States Supreme Court has sided with the police that discretion is necessary to be effective. This is a wonderful thing for us! Even more so, we must do our part so this remains the case. If we abuse it by making unnecessary arrests and enforcement, it can easily become more limited and greatly affect our ability to do our job.

"Discretion is our greatest tool and our greatest liability."

Increased mutual respect and understanding will be necessary for successful policing in the 21st century. As you can imagine, opinions are abundant about both sides of this encounter. The fact is that there is no denying that sharp differences remain between police and their communities. *Both* the police and citizens will have to work at improving these matters to gain a mutual respect, appreciation, and trust that will result in increased police support through improved community relations. Again, the only part you can control is YOU. Be excellent!

CHAPTER 10 EXCELLENCE KEYS

➢ Someone must be the adult in the room; tag, you're it. The community expects YOU to be the adult in the room.

➢ Sometimes potentially dangerous encounters dictate that procedural justice be applied after a threat is diminished. Taking the time to explain why you took certain actions at the end is just as effective as if it were practiced in the middle (remember the Process).

➢ Just because you can do something legally doesn't mean it's necessary.

➢ Discretion is our greatest tool and our greatest liability.

➢ When making the best decision, ask yourself, *"What does the result look like? What is the win?"*

➢ Increased mutual respect and understanding will be necessary for policing in the 21st century.

CHAPTER 11

A FEW MORE DETAILS
CYNICISM, SARCASM, AND EMPATHY

Along the way, we've learned both good and bad habits. Perhaps you've become a bit more robotic in your daily behavior towards citizens or maybe all calls have become the same to you. "Same ol' shit, different day" you may say. It happens. Self-reflection is another important aspect of being excellent. If you don't take the time to take a step back to see your real self, then it will be difficult to become a better version of you. You must know where you are now before you get to where you want to be. That is, of course, if you want to improve.

Ken Blanchard said, "Feedback is the breakfast of champions." Surround yourself with people you trust who will speak the truth to you. People are like elevators; they'll either take you up or bring you down. Guess which group people of excellence surround themselves with. Start changing any negative behavior and turn your bad habits into good ones.

I've certainly changed over the past twenty plus years in policing. I am sure you have too. Like most of you, I came into this profession wanting to help others. Heck, that's what most of us said in our preliminary interviews when asked this same question. "Why do you want to be a police officer?" And we sat there, a bit naïve, and responded the same way, "I want to help people." I can still see the half smirks on the faces of my panel members as they tried to maintain their poker faces. That was cynicism radiating from their faces. You and I understand that now. It happens. Cynicism is one pitfall to be aware of as you strive to be excellent in policing.

CYNICISM

"Every ounce of my cynicism is supported by historical precedent."
Glen Cook

It seems the longer one is in law enforcement, the more cynical he/she becomes. That bright eyed and bushy tailed younger person you used to be that came into law enforcement has faded away. What the hell happened? I heard one high level commander say, "policing would be a fantastic job if it weren't for the people!" Police officers understand that. Screenwriter Lillian Hellman said, "Cynicism is an unpleasant way of saying the truth."[xxxv] Then there's this follow up question, "What is truth?" Maybe cynicism is an unpleasant way of speaking partial truths because there are usually some of it in cynicism. As police officers, you should consistently challenge what *your* truth is.

I do believe that part *of learning* is *unlearning*. People believe what they repeatedly hear and see. Police officers constantly deal with situations and people that are challenging, to say the least. You answer calls for service that can be argued shouldn't have been dispatched in the first place. You deal with the very small percentage of people that don't necessarily like the police. Officers deal with people who lie to them frequently, and the list goes on. Merriam–Webster defines *cynicism* as a belief that people are generally selfish and dishonest.[xxxvi] It's no wonder that officers become cynical over time. Here's the pitfall: Police officers can begin believing that *everyone* lies to them and everyone doesn't like them. So naturally, over time, it becomes easier to treat citizens differently. Officers build the proverbial wall around themselves, and it's difficult for officers to see past it, much less allow anyone to get close to them. This can result in showing lack of compassion and diminish citizens' satisfaction of the police.

I appreciate how Dr. Kevin Gilmartin, author of "Emotional Survival for Law Enforcement," describes how police officers perceive the world. He says everything is "bullshit" and those who cause it are "assholes." And I haven't even started talking about the internal departmental "bullshit." The internal BS may be the worst part of the job! By the way, I encourage you to read Dr. Gilmartin's book- it will help you.

Here's the bottom line- people still need YOU- a real human being who believes in and represents the best of humanity. Cynics expect the worst in others. Most people really do want to do the right thing. May your attitude and actions continue to encourage them to keep doing so. We should be the example. Do not allow cynicism to get the best of you. There is no room for it in your journey towards excellence.

SARCASM

If you've been married for more than one week, you know for a fact that sarcasm hurts. Being sarcastic can be extremely hurtful to the recipient. The adage about 'sticks and stones can break my bones, but words will never hurt me' is a bunch of bullshit. Words hurt, especially coming from someone you love and trust.

Officers tend to develop this trait over time. Some may cope from the daily grind by being sarcastic to others. Officers have thick skin for the most part, so joking around with other police officers can seem to be okay for the most part. However, sarcasm lances through tough skin eventually, even with your peers.

Being sarcastic with your citizens is never appropriate. One definition of sarcasm is "a sharp and often satirical or ironic utterance designed to cut or give pain." [xxxvii] Wow, it's designed to give pain! No wonder it cuts like a knife. King David in Psalms 59:7NIV wrote, "See what they spew from their mouths— the words from their lips are sharp as swords." If you prefer the King James Version, "Behold, they belch out with their mouth: swords are in their lips." Your words are more powerful than you may believe.

The etymology of the word sarcasm is enlightening. The first part *'sarc'* or *'sarx'* in the Greek language infers to tearing of the flesh. [xxxviii] I know, I'm starting to sound like the dad in the movie *My Big Fat Greek Wedding*. It is thought-provoking though. The second part of the word is *-casm*, or *chasm*. Merriam Webster defines a chasm as a deep divide, a separation, or difference. So, sarcasm is a tearing of the flesh causing a deep divide. Ok, I've beaten this horse enough, but you get the point. Sarcasm hurts others.

Now let's try and look at this from a citizen's perspective that has been spoken to sarcastically by a police officer. If people view the police as a legitimate authority, visualize how sarcasm can violate that trust that those you serve have placed in you. Sarcasm can undermine our efforts to gain more trust and confidence in us. Plus, I'm trying to save you some grief here; sarcasm will get you nothing but a complaint. It can negatively impact your career, your department, and your city.

EMPATHY

Sympathy and empathy are not the same. I read this and appreciate the way this writer summed up the difference: "Sympathy is feeling compassion, sorrow, or pity for the hardships that another person encounters, while empathy is placing yourself in the shoes of another." [xxxix]

Showing compassion is a community expectation. Officers should show more of it when interacting with citizens. Doing so is good business because it communicates that you care, understand, and have a genuine servant's heart and mind.

There are times, however, when officers can show empathy when appropriate. Again, I am not stating you must cry with or hug every citizen you meet. I am, however, saying that it is more than okay to hurt alongside the community when something tragic occurs in your city.

Expressing empathy can be as simple as quietly attending a funeral or vigil service for a community member. It can be you writing a heartfelt message on a card or, even better, a handwritten letter to those who are hurting. Consider this, when an officer is seriously hurt or, God forbid, killed in the line of duty, the community always shows their support in an extraordinary way. They hurt alongside us in our time of deep sorrow and grief. Citizens want to do something for officers to help them get through the toughest of times. That is *community* in every sense of the word.

Conversely, when something heartbreaking occurs in your city, why shouldn't your police department hurt alongside with those who are hurting? Yes, officers still must remain professional to do their job, especially during those tough times, but there are times that demand more than just doing your job. Expressing empathy shows those we serve that we can walk in their shoes and hurt with them in their time of need as well. This is community.

Chapter 11 Excellence Keys

- Self-reflection is an important aspect of excellence.

- Surround yourself with people who can speak truth to you about yourself.

- Part of *learning* is *unlearning*. People believe what they repeatedly hear and see.

- *Cynicism* is a belief that people are generally selfish and dishonest.

- Don't allow your cynicism to control your citizen encounters. People still need YOU- a real human being who still believes in and represents the best of humanity.

- The adage about 'sticks and stones can break my bones, but words will never hurt me' is a bunch of bullshit. Words hurt; especially coming from someone you love and trust.

- *Sarcasm* is a tearing of the flesh causing a deep divide.

- Sarcasm can violate the trust that those you serve have placed in you.

- *Sympathy* is feeling compassion, sorrow, or pity for the hardships that another person encounters, while empathy is placing yourself in the shoes of another.

- Expressing empathy shows those we serve that we can walk in their shoes and hurt with them in their time of need.

Chapter 12

Parting Thoughts

An instructor I know would end his classes with this question, "So what?" I'll ask you the same thing, "So what?" There's no doubt that policing today is challenging to say the least. It seems as if the world has turned their backs on you. They haven't. Imagine a world without police officers and how different our nation would be. People still depend on you.

We will never be perfect, but we can certainly be excellent. Being excellent keeps us moving in the right direction; if we're not moving forward, then you're moving backwards; there are no neutral gears. Excellence is in the details, or little matters. Let's focus on the importance of managing the details of every citizen encounter. We must replace the checker board with a chess board.

Building police legitimacy helps the police do their job easier and, more importantly, be safer. We should do everything in our control to protect the legitimacy we are privileged to have now but also continue to look for ways to increase it. We learned that one way of building legitimacy is by practicing procedural justice during every encounter. The more procedural justice is used, the more legitimacy is built. The more legitimacy you've earned, the more authority you have. The more authority (influence) you possess, the less power you will have to use, and that's a good thing!

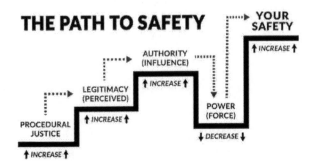

I am honored that you took the time to read and finish the book. My hope is that you take a few things to consider as you move forward in your law enforcement career.

May every one of your commercials be worthy to be aired during the Super Bowl to show the world who we really are. Thank you for representing the best in people and choosing to be excellent in all you do!

God Bless You,

Andy Harvey

REFERENCES

[i] Alexander Alekhine Quotes. (n.d.). Retrieved February 11, 2018, from
https://www.brainyquote.com/authors/alexander_alekhine

[ii] Objective. (n.d.). Retrieved February 11, 2018, from
http://www.dictionary.com/browse/objective?s=t

[iii] Excellence Quotes. (n.d.). Retrieved February 11, 2018, from
https://www.brainyquote.com/topics/excellence

[iv] Zimring, F. E. (2009). *The great American crime decline.* New York: Oxford
University Press.

[v] A. (n.d.). Quote about excellence by Aristotle on Quotations Book. Retrieved
February 11, 2018, from http://quotationsbook.com/quote/12996/

[vi] Collins, J. (2011) Good to Great. New York, NY: HarperCollins Publishers Inc.
page 247-248

[vii] Collins, J. (2011) Good to Great. New York, NY: HarperCollins Publishers Inc.
page 71-72

[viii] BibleGateway. (n.d.). Retrieved February 11, 2018, from
https://www.biblegateway.com/passage/?search=Philippians%2B3&ve
rsion=ESV strain forward

[ix] Gallup- Americans' Respect for Police Surges. (n.d.). Retrieved from
http://news.gallup.com/poll/196610/americans-respect-police-
surges.aspx?version=print

[x] Retrieved from http://www.gallup.com/poll/1654/Honesty-Ethics-Professions
.aspx?g_source=honesty%20and%20ethical%20standards%20of%20pe
ople%20in%20these%20d&g_medium=search&g_campaign=tiles

[xi] Tyler, T. R. (2006). *Why people obey the law.* Princeton, NJ: Princeton
University Press. P. 3-5

[xii] Meares, Tracey L., "Norms, Legitimacy and Law Enforcement" (2000).
Faculty Scholarship Series. 515. P. 403
http://digitalcommons.law.yale.edu/fss_papers/515

xiii (n.d.). Retrieved from https:fifthdown.blogs.nytimes.com/2009/03/30/dallas-Police-officer-makes-death-even-worse/

xiv Dictionary by Merriam-Webster: America's most-trusted online dictionary. (n.d.). Retrieved February 11, 2018, from https://www.merriam-webster.com/dictionary/common%20sense

xv (n.d.). Retrieved from http://www.thefreedictionary.com/delegate

xvi President's Task Force on 21st Century Policing. (n.d.). Retrieved from https://content.umuc.edu/file/bb062e55-1570-4f42-b4ea-ea152eb56a2c/1/FinalReportofthePresidentsTaskForceon21stCenturyPolicing.pdf

xvii Police Executive Research Forum-(2014) Legitimacy and Procedural Justice: A New Element of Police Leadership P.9) http://www.policeforum.org/assets/docs/Free_Online_Documents/Leadership/legitimacy%20and%20procedural%20justice%20-%20a%20new%20element%20of%20police%20leadership.pdf

xviii (n.d.). Retrieved from https://www.academia.edu/7762939/Trust_in_the_Police_The_influence_of_procedural_justice_and_perceived_collective_efficacy p.4

xix Meares, Tracey L., "Norms, Legitimacy and Law Enforcement" (2000). *Faculty Scholarship Series*. 515. P. 403 http://digitalcommons.law.yale.edu/fss_papers/515

xx Weisburd, D., & Braga, A. A. (2008). *Police innovation: contrasting perspectives*. Cambridge: Cambridge University Press. P. 254

xxi Weisburd, D., & Braga, A. A. (2008). *Police innovation: contrasting perspectives*. Cambridge: Cambridge University Press. P. 255

xxii Tyler, T. R. (2006). *Why people obey the law*. Princeton, NJ: Princeton University Press. P. 4

xxiii Tyler, T. R. (2006). *Why people obey the law*. Princeton, NJ: Princeton University Press.

xxiv Weisburd, D., & Braga, A. A. (2008). *Police innovation: contrasting perspectives*. Cambridge: Cambridge University Press. P. 253

xxv Weisburd, D., & Braga, A. A. (2008). *Police innovation: contrasting perspectives*. Cambridge: Cambridge University Press.

xxvi Respect. (n.d.). Retrieved February 13, 2018, from https://www.merriam-webster.com/dictionary/respect

xxvii Yahoo Health. (2015, June 18). Science Reveals How to Make Yourself Appear More Trustworthy. Retrieved February 13, 2018, from https://www.yahoo.com/beauty/science-reveals-how-to-make-yourself-appear-more-121846659297.html

xxviii Legitimacy and Procedural Justice: A New Element of Police Leadership A Report by the Police Executive Research Forum (PERF). (2014, March P. 8). Retrieved February 13, 2018, from http://www.policeforum.org/assets/docs/Free_Online_Documents/Leadership/legitimacy%20and%20procedural%20justice%20-%20a%20new%20element%20of%20police%20leadership.pdf

xxix BADGE OF LIFE FAQS. (n.d.). Retrieved February 13, 2018, from http://www.badgeoflife.com/badge-life-faqs/

xxx (n.d.). Retrieved from http://www2.cambridgema.gov/CityOfCambridge_Content/documents/Cambridge%20Review_FINAL.pdf P. 21

xxxi (n.d.). Retrieved from http://www2.cambridgema.gov/CityOfCambridge_Content/documents/Cambridge%20Review_FINAL.pdf P. 3

xxxii (n.d.). Retrieved from http://www2.cambridgema.gov/CityOfCambridge_Content/documents/Cambridge%20Review_FINAL.pdf P. 4

xxxiii (n.d.). Retrieved from http://www2.cambridgema.gov/CityOfCambridge_Content/documents/Cambridge%20Review_FINAL.pdf P. 21

xxxiv (n.d.). Retrieved from http://www2.cambridgema.gov/CityOfCambridge_Content/documents/Cambridge%20Review_FINAL.pdf P. 21

xxxv Cynicism Quotes. (n.d.). Retrieved February 13, 2018, from http://www.brainyquote.com/quotes/keywords/cynicism.html

xxxvi Cynicism. (n.d.). Retrieved February 13, 2018, from
http://www.merriam-webster.com/dictionary/cynicism

xxxvi Sarcasm. (n.d.). Retrieved February 13, 2018, from
http://www.merriam-webster.com/dictionary/sarcasm

xxxvi Content: Isaac Mozeson / Website Developer: Daniel David. (n.d.). Edenics
(Biblical Hebrew). Retrieved February 13, 2018, from
http://www.edenics.net/english-word-origins.aspx?word=SARCASM

xxxvi (n.d.). Retrieved from (n.d.). Retrieved February 13, 2018, from
https://www.bing.com/search?q=difference%2Bbetween%2Bsympathy
%2Band%2Bempathy&go=Submit&qs=n&form=CHRDEF&pc=U480
&pq=difference%2Bbetween%2Bsympathy%2Band%2Bempathy&sc=5
-39&sp=-1&sk=&cvid=A2D12E0B45C84B76A3C77EB0DCD570BA

Made in the USA
Middletown, DE
28 March 2019